KNOCK 'EM DEAD

THE TALENT SHOW FROM HELL!

A YOU-SOLVE-IT COMEDY

by

Tom Oldendick & Will Roberson

SAMUEL FRENCH, INC.

45 West 25th Street	NEW YORK 10010
7623 Sunset Boulevard	HOLLYWOOD 90046
LONDON	*TORONTO*

IMPORTANT BILLING AND CREDIT
REQUIREMENTS

All producers of *KNOCK 'EM DEAD* *must* give credit to the Author of the Play in all programs distributed in connection with performances of the Play and in all instances in which the title of the Play appears for purposes of advertising, publicizing or otherwise exploiting the Play and/or a production. The name of the Author *must* also appear on a separate line, on which no other name appears, immediately following the title, and *must* appear in size of type not less than fifty percent the size of the title type.

Knock 'Em Dead premiered at the Phoenix Little Theatre in June, 1990. It was directed by Will Roberson; the set was designed by Tom Oldendick, the costumes by Valeria Watson, the lighting by Brian Morphew and had the following cast (in order of appearance):

LOU DUMBELLO .... Steven A. Fried
HAL BROWN .... Charles Keever
ROXIE BARN .... Celeste Dignoti
BAMBY LYNN .... Lisa Martina
IAN WAYNE .... Robert Locke
LOTTA VERBOTEN .... Susan Miller-Dee
GREAT SOMNAMBULO .... Mark Buckner
VINNIE BUMPCUSS.............. George Spelvin

<h1 style="text-align:center">CHARACTERS</h1>
(in order of appearance)

LOU DUMBELLO: Vinnie's MC and general flunky, he once sang like a bird but after ten years at Vinnie's Club his voice has flown the coop.

HAL BROWN: A ventriloquist with more to hide than moving lips. His case contains a dummy that can really shoot off its mouth.

ROXY BARN: A stand-up comic with an attitude as rotten as her life. Where she comes from they didn't call her "Rocky" for nothing.

BAMBY LYNN: A blond with measurements higher than her IQ. She thinks doing the splits is a talent. One look at her and you know why she won.

"IAN" WAYNE: A little fairy with eyes to make it big in show-biz with his tutti-frutti dog act and if anyone gets in his way they better watch out, he was named after the "Duke."

LOTTA VERBOTEN: A chanteuse who's been kept locked away from society, but now she's out and she's singing the blues.

The GREAT SOMNAMBULO: A hypnotist who can put an entire room to sleep by just talking to them. His turban hides more than Grecian Formula.

VINNIE: A second-rate hood, the only thing oilier than him is his cheap toupee.

PLACE

Vinnie's Belly Laugh Club on the south side of any city in the US. Vinne's is one of those clubs where you go when you're desperate for entertainment or desperate for a job. It's early evening on a rainy Tuesday, the night of the finals for Vinnie's talent search. The winner of tonight's competition will win a four-week contract to headline at the club and a check for a $1,000.

SET

The storage area off the back alley entrance that serves as a "green room" for the waiting performers. DR is the passage to the club and the stage. UC in the back wall are two doors, one leads to Vinne's office, the other one is to the only washroom. Between the two doors on the wall is a pay phone surrounded with phone numbers. DL is the only door to the outside. Stacks of beer cases line the walls, leaning against the wall is a step ladder. A folding card table, an old folding chair and a run-down sofa are the only furniture. A bright new sandwich board sign proclaiming VINNIE'S Talent Competition Finals TONIGHT! leans against some of the beer cases.

ACT I

(HOUSE LIGHTS are at half.)

VOICE OVER. (*Thunder.*) It was too dark, too hot and too wet. A shroud of rain hung over the city and threatened to foreclose on the south side of town. Violence boiled up from the steaming asphalt and hovered in the air like an unpaid bill. At Vinnie's, a motley crowd of desperate suspects was gathering for a seemingly innocent talent show. Tonight, one of them will collect on an old debt, while another one pays the price. A crime is about to happen, keep your eyes peeled, anything you see may be used against them.

(LOU comes in nervously jiggling the change in his pocket, frantically puffing on the end of a cigar. HE turns on more LIGHTS, checks his watch, sets up card table and chairs, drops a chair, [BANG] thinks it's a gun shot, raises hands, hides behind couch, realizes it wasn't a shot. Goes to the phone, dials a number, no answer, slams receiver ... nervously HE puts in more coins, looks at a number on the wall, dials, busy, slams receiver down. Checking his watch again, HE goes to the door to Vinnie's office, tries the knob, it's locked, HE raps on the door.)

LOU. Vinnie, Vinnie, I gotta talk to you.
VINNIE. (*From behind door.*) Not now, I'm busy.

LOU. You're always busy. *(Exits into club.)*

(HAL enters through the alley door carrying a large black suitcase. HE shakes the rain off his coat and hat. Nervously HE checks to make sure he's alone and begins casing the place. HE goes to Vinnie's door and listens; nothing; HE hears a sound, HE's jumpy, HE pulls a gun from his coat pocket, crouches down and pulls open the door to the washroom, empty, HE turns to go to the club, HE hears LOU coming back. HAL jumps and hides in the washroom, LOU comes in singing just as HAL closes the door.)

LOU. *(Enters, checks a number on the wall and looking around to make sure he's alone dials the number, lets it ring for a long time and hangs up, goes to office door.)* Vinnie, you only got a coupla hours to come up with the dough or there's going to be real trouble around here. Vinnie, you listening? *(Checking his watch nervously.)* There ain't much time left, Vinnie; let me go on tonight, you promised. I know I can make it work, listen ... O sole mio. I could tell a couple of jokes ... Vinnie, Vinnie ... Ah SHIT! *(LOU picks up the sandwich board sign and exits into the club.)*

(HAL emerges from washroom with his gun drawn and ready for action and is surprised to see the room is empty. HE starts towards Vinnie's door when the PHONE rings. HE freezes, it RINGS again. Looking both ways in panic HE lunges for the phone and answers it.)

HAL. (*Frantic.*) Belly Laugh Club. (*Pause.*) No, he's not here right now. (*Pause.*) Ah ...   this is a ... (*Desperately looking around HE sees the beer cases.*) Bud ... Bud Weiser ... man ... OK I'll give him the message. (*HE hangs up.*)

LOU. (*Enters from the club just as Hal hangs up the phone.*) HEY! What are you up to?

HAL. (*With his back to Lou slips the gun into his coat and turns.*) No one was here, I was just answering the phone. (*Moving towards Lou with his hand extended.*) The talent agency sent me over, I'm Hal Brown ... the ventriloquist? ... you know, for tonight's show.... (*Picking up case to show the names.*) "WEN Y & HAL, the comedy act that answers the WHO and WHAT of your entertainment needs."

LOU. Talent, at Vinnie's? Now that's a laugh. we didn't order no talent ... and who was on the phone?

HAL. Oh, that was just a wrong number. You must have ordered some talent for tonight. I got the message right here ... (*Fumbling with message from his pocket.*) ... from the Star Light, Star Bright First Star I See Tonight Talent Agency. (*Reading.*) "Vinne's Belly Laugh, two shows, Wednesday night 8 pm. Try to be funny this time. Sheri." See?

LOU. Yeh, that's great, but tonight's TUESDAY not WEDNESDAY and tonight is the big finals of VINNE'S ANNUAL TALENT SEARCH, so in a few minutes we're going to be up to our asses in FREE talent and believe me with these acts the last thing we need is more talking dummys. So buzz off and tell Sheri at Twinkle, Twinkle Little Talent Agency we ain't paying for no talent tonight.

You're a day early and out of luck. (*Starts showing Hal to the door.*)

HAL. Wait a second. We haven't got any place to go and it's raining. We had friends drop us off. They're coming back to see the show, can't we just wait here until they come back? Or better yet, can't we be in the competition?

LOU. (*Becoming exasperated.*) Look, I told ya these are the finals, the competition is over. There are five finalists due here any minute, each of 'em's hoping to win. The first prize ... (*With pride.*) ... is a thousand smackers and four weeks as the head chuckle here at Vinnie's Belly Laugh.

HAL. (*Looking around at the room. As Wendall.*) So what's second prize, you don't have to play at the Club?

LOU. Very funny, at Vinnie's everyone's a comedian. Your dummy's jokes are better than yours. (*HAL is taking Wendell out of the case.*) You can't be in the competition and neither can the talking two by four. But if ya want to stick around and talk with Vinnie, it's OK with me.

(*Alley door bursts open, and in comes ROXIE BARN.*)

ROXIE. (*Shaking rain off her coat.*) Jeez, what a night, it rains once a year in this dump and He ... (*Looking up to heaven.*) ... picks tonight, what a pisser. Hey, haven't you ever seen a lady before? Help me off with this cheap rain coat before it shrinks up and strangles me.

HAL. Allow me.

(*HE helps ROXIE out of her wet coat and looks around, handing her coat on the hook on inside of UC door.*)

LOU. You're the stand-up comic, right? The one with all of the four-letter words. I remember you.

ROXIE. Yeah, that's me, Roxie Barn, B-A-R-N, that's a four-letter word that's guaranteed to get laughs. With this crowd anything more than four letters and it's over their heads. They move their lips to read a stop sign.

HAL. You never see my lips move. (*Covering mouth.*) I mean you never see my lips move.

ROXIE. What do you do for an encore, the dummy drinks water and you spit up?

HAL. (*To dummy.*) She's seen our act!

ROXIE. That was a joke.

LOU. Great. Well the show, I mean the finals don't start until nine and you're the first to arrive. Give it a rest, I've got to check some things out front. (*HE exits into club.*)

ROXIE. (*Picking up empty beer cans.*) Budweiser! They redecorated. Who are YOU? The bathroom attendant in this toilet? (*SHE sits on up-ended beer case.*)

HAL. No, Miss Barn, I'm Hal ... of "Wen Y & Hal."

ROXIE. Who and what?

HAL. You heard of us! WEN Y & HAL. "The who and what of your entertainment needs." No group too large or too small. You've seen our act?

ROXIE. No and I hope to keep my eyes closed tonight. You're my competition?

HAL. No, Miss Barn, we're here by mistake.

ROXIE. Truer words were never spoken. (*Looking around.*) Where's the rest of the yous, whos and whats? They go out for a drink without me?

HAL. No Miss Barn, it's just me and Wendell. Wendell's my partner, and dummy.

ROXIE. Sounds like my last three husbands. I wish I could have locked them in a suitcase. (*SHE knocks on Wendell's head.*) And they were never this hard.

HAL. (*Covering Wendell's ears.*) Don't listen to her, Wendell.

ROXIE. Afraid Wendell's gonna get a Woody?

(The alley door blows open and in comes BAMBY with an equipment bag and holding a newspaper over her head.)

BAMBY. Oh gosh, I hope my hair isn't ruined, I spent all afternoon under a hot hair dresser ... Oh—(*Seeing Hal and Roxie.*)—I mean a hair dryer. A girl can't be too careful about her looks, especially the ones she gets from guys. (*Giggles. Looking around, SHE moves C and spells out her name with her body shaped like each letter.*) READY, OK. I'm Bamby Lynn, Bamby with a "Y." B-A-M-B-Y. Bamby with a "Y."

ROXIE. Bamby with a "Y"? No wonder Disney killed your mother.

BAMBY. (*Looking around the room.*) He did!?! (*Giggle.*) Are these the dressing rooms? (*Looking into WC.*) Is it co-ed?

ROXIE. Looks that way. Just stow it where ever you can find some space. (*SHE watches BAMBY drag her bag across the floor.*) What've you got in there, an entire beauty shop or are you moonlighting for Mary Kay?

BAMBY. (*Opening the suitcase.*) Oh, no, just a few things that every girl needs and the props for my act. I came in my costume. (*SHE opens her coat to reveal a a stripper's body in a glitzy, skimpy cheerleader outfit.*) See!

ROXIE. We can see everything but your bank balance. What do you do in that getup, the entire football team?

BAMBY. You're so clever, you got it right away. (*Taking off her coat.*) This is for my salute to "American pastimes that use balls"!

ROXIE. Oh great, you got an inflatable man in there?

BAMBY. (*Taking the balls out of the bag as if to juggle them.*) No, silly, footballs, basketballs and baseballs.

ROXIE. Hold it! Hold it, I know this place is a gutter but if you pull a bowling ball out of there I'm pushing the reset button. That's your act? Demonstrating sports equipment.

WENDELL. If you like croquet, Bamby, I've got wooden balls ... (*HAL claps hand over Wendell's mouth.*)

ROXIE. If you're any example of the other finalists they can just give me that check now.

BAMBY. Well, don't be so sure. I always wow them with my spectacular end. It's patriotic and full of enthusiasm. (*SHE goes into baton twirl and ends in a split.*)

ROXIE. My God, she's stuck. Give me a hand, Hal, we gotta rock'er back and forth to break the suction.

BAMBY. I'm fine ... (*ROXIE is helping her up.*) ... really.

ROXIE. (*Looking at the floor.*) Stripped the wax right off the floor.

BAMBY. Say, you didn't tell me your name.

ROXIE. I'm Roxie Barn, the comic.

BAMBY. Oh, not *the* Roxie Barn? (*Thinking for a second.*) Never heard of you. I'm sure that after tonight they are going to know my name, Miz Barn. Once they see my big finales. (*Doing one leg stand with two flags.*)

LOU. (*Entering from club.*) Now that's what I call talent. We won't can that.

(*Alley door flies open and in comes IAN, laden with boxes and costumes, wearing an outrageously flashy costume from a bad ice show.*)

IAN. (*Non-stop as HE distributes his things around the room.*) I thought I was going to have to build an ark to get here. Thank God, I wrapped everything ... if the maribou gets wet my act is washed up ... and it wouldn't be pretty. Hold these, honey ... Thank God for plastic it may not be biodegradable but it's all in the service of my art ... only a few more things ... I'll be right back .... at least moisture is good for the complexion. Don't rain on my parade ... (*Exits.*)

BAMBY. What was that?

ROXIE. Liberace's love child?

BAMBY. Really?!?

LOU. No that's last week's winner, his act is a dog.

ROXIE. Like hers isn't.

LOU. No, a real dog, you know, woof woof. OK, who's here so far? (*Pointing to Roxie.*) We got the comic, (*Lifting one of Ian's high heels.*) we got Imelda Marcos and her talking dog act, and we got the real talent, (*Pinching Bamby's bottom.*) the meat of the show; that leaves the hypnotist and the blues singer ... blues singers are always late.

(LOTTA enters on Lou's last line.)

LOTTA. *(In a thick quasi German accent.)* Most men enjoy waiting for Lotta Verboten. De blues singer has arrived ... *(Sings a line from a song appropriate to the moment.)* ... To whom do I give my music to?

LOU. I'll take it out front to the piano player and check your mike ... Singers!!! See ya later, Bamby.

IAN. *(Entering with folding screen and Fifi.)* Fifi was just terrified out there in the car ... I hope her nerves aren't frayed, she's such an artist, she's so sensitive like Marilyn Monroe and you know what happened to her ... stay away from those Kennedys, Fifi ... You know you can never be too careful with a star.

LOTTA. You're making me dizzy ... *(IAN misses Lotta with the screen.)* Hey! Watch it with that thing.

IAN. What? *(Turning and barely missing Bamby.)*

ROXIE. Watch where you're going, girlie.

IAN. Huh? What? *(Turning in confusion, HE smacks Bamby in the ass with the screen, sending her flying face forward on her hands. Major chaos.)*

BAMBY. *(Screams.)* Oh my wrists, *my* wrists!

IAN. *(To Fifi.)* Oh, sweety, are you all right!?

BAMBY. I think I sprained my wrist ...

IAN. Darling precious, did that strange lady scare you?

ROXIE. Don't try to pin it on me, Tinkerbell. But I think you knocked Miss Congeniality here out of the competition.

IAN. Oh, dear, I'm so sorry. *(Going to Bamby.)* Are you hurt?

BAMBY. OUT OF THE COMPETITION! If my wrists swell up my career is over.

ROXIE. There is a God.

LOTTA. (*Singing.*) "Amazing grace how sweet thou art...."

BAMBY. I won't be able to twirl or anything, get me some ice. Quick!

LOTTA. Oh darling don't worry. (*Singing a line from a song appropriate to the moment.*)

BAMBY. ICE! Get me some ICE.

IAN. (*Hysteria setting in.*) ICE! Yes, ice ... You hold Fifi while I play nursey. You be good until Mama gets back. (*HE exits into club. Offstage.*) Ice, ice, ice!!!!

ROXIE. Hurry back, we wouldn't want Fifi to get lonely. This powderpuff with an attitude is bad for my image. (*Looking around ROXIE puts Fifi in pre-rigged escapable beer case.*)

BAMBY. (*Dropping to her knees and holding her wrists.*) They're swelling! They're swelling! I'll never twirl again.

ROXIE. You better get up before the Ice Capades get back. There's nothing worse than a dizzy flaming fruit with a mission.

HAL. (*Who has been watching with interest from his chair.*) If you raise her arms above her head her wrists won't swell. (*HE demonstrates with Wendell's arms.*)

ROXIE. (*Raises Bamby's arms up in the air over her head.*) Here honey, it's worth a try.

(*Just then LOU rushes in and sees everyone with their arms in the air and thinking the worst, puts his arms up too.*)

LOU. (*In a panic.*) Don't shoot, don't shoot ... Vinnie, the jig's up ... It's not me you want ... I'm just the MC. (*Grabbing LOTTA and backing out of the room.*) You wouldn't shoot a lady ... (*Pulling her dress out in front.*) ... and she's pregnant ....

IAN. (*Running in with ice bucket.*) The Ice Man Cometh! (*HE runs into Lou's back and the ice goes flying.*)

LOU. (*Feeling the impact of the ice bucket.*) They got me! I've been shot! I've been shot! Tell Vinnie it wasn't me, I'm not a stoolie ... I'm coming, Mama ... (*Falling to the floor and flopping over on his back.*) I'm kicking the bucket!

LOTTA. (*Sings a line from a song appropriate to the moment.*)

ROXIE. Cut the act! The only bucket you're kicking is the ice bucket. You're not shot.

LOU. (*Recovering sheepishly.*) I'm not? I'm not! I knew it all the time, I was just foolin' around. What's going on here, what happened anyway?

BAMBY. I was doing my finale when out of nowhere I saw stars. I think I've got a NA VIC U LAR SPRAIN with CAR PAL TUNNEL SYNDROME, oh God. (*Holding out her hands.*) PARAS THESIS is setting in. (*EVERYONE stops and stares at Bamby. Realizing what she has said SHE reverts back to her dizzy self.*) What will I do if they start to turn blue?

ROXIE. Paint your arms red and white and wave 'em for old glory. I can never pass up a good punch line.

IAN. I'm so sorry. I'm sure you will be just fine. I've got to bring in the rest of my things while it's not raining. You know how easily rhinestones get water spots. (*Exits.*)

LOTTA. (*Trying to clear her throat and sing. SHE sings a line from a song appropriate to the moment. Cough.*) This rain is no good for my voice.

ROXIE. The only thing good for your voice would be laryngitis.

LOTTA. (*Dropping accent.*) I'll have you know ... sister, I was strictly SRO at the convent.

BAMBY, then HAL and WENDELL, then ROXIE. The convent?

LOTTA. (*Regaining accent and composure.*) Oh, that's a little club I used to play in Toledo.

LOU. You singing the same songs as last time?

LOTTA. Of course, my medley of highlights from the *Sound of Music*.

ROXIE. The *Sound of Music*! Oh, brother, between you and Miss Hills Are Alive over there, the deck is stacked in my favor.

LOTTA. (*Singing in her sexiest voice a line appropriate to the moment.*)

IAN. (*Entering with third load of things.*) Gangway, girls, move it or lose it, I don't want to knock anyone else out of the competition. Only kidding. I think I have everything. Let's see, (*Looking into shopping bag and pulling out each item.*) Silly String, Ravel's "Bolero," "Knife Throwing Made Easy" ... (*EVERYONE stops and looks at IAN who drops the book back in his bag.*) ... and Fifi's first-act costume. (*Looking around frantically.*) FIFI! Where's FIFI!!? What have you done to her? Where's my FIFI?

ROXIE. Don't get your panties in a wad, he's ...

IAN. SHE! Fifi is a SHE! Show business is in her blood, I'll have you know her grandmother sat on Gloria Swanson's lap.

ROXIE. Big deal. My grandfather sat on Gloria Swanson's face.

IAN. (*Pause.*) Ya got me there.

ROXIE. (*Bringing over the beer case with Fifi in it.*) Here, her royal hiney is right here. (*Handing case to Ian.*) See for yourself, all safe and sound.

IAN. (*Looking into case with horror.*) She's DEAD! (*Holding up a limp paw.*) You've killed her! She's suffocated to death! CALL 911, call 911 (*Grabs phone and hands it to LOTTA.*) Call 911! OH Fifi! (*Tries mouth to mouth.*) ... She's not responding. Look at her just laying there ...

ROXIE. (*Looking in case.*) Before you try the Heimlich maneuver, get over it. She's fine, she just drank up some spilt beer, she's not dead, she's ...

IAN. (*In a snit.*) DRUNK! Fifi's DRUNK! You got her drunk! Oh Fifi, and she's a minor ... you got her drunk on purpose ... to ruin my act!

LOTTA. (*Coming between Roxie and Ian.*) If you girls will excuse me, I think I'll sit this one out. (*Singing a line from a song appropriate to the moment. SHE enters washroom and closes the door.*)

IAN. (*Still fuming.*) That's it! Now I see it! You're jealous. You got Fifi drunk and you made me knock this wholesome all-American girl onto her patriotic little fanny. You're terrified of anyone with real talent.

ROXIE. Get over it. The day I have to sabotage acts like this to win a cheap talent contest is the day I hang it up. Look at you. (*Indicating Lotta in WC.*) We've got

Julie Andrews trapped in Eva Braun's body … (*To Bamby.*) … an over-the-hill flaming baton act … (*To Ian.*) … and a run-of-the-mill flaming … dog act. All we need now is …

SOMNAMBULO. (*Whirls through the door with a theatrical flair.*) The GREAT SOMNAMBULO! Hypnotist extraodinaire. You may commence grovelling.

ROXIE. Trapped in the Twilight Zone!

LOTTA. (*Singing Twilight Zone theme from the WC.*) DOODOO DOODOO DOODOO.

ROXIE. Tonight's episode, "The Talent Show From Hell."

SOMNAMBULO. (*Moving across room.*) Do I feel tension? (*To Roxie.*) I feel desperate and dateless. (*To the door of the WC.*) I feel a song coming on? (*To Ian.*) I feel dizzy.

ROXIE. (*Confronting Somnambulo.*) I feel a fraud!

LOU. (*Entering from club.*) Great, you're all here. I see you've all met, nice to see you're all getting along so well. Where's the kraut?

ROXIE. She's in the can.

LOTTA. (*Sound of TOILET flush, then LOTTA comes out of the WC with large piece of toilet paper stuck to her shoe and singing a line from a song appropriate to the moment.*)

LOU. Has Vinnie been out to talk wit'ya yet?

EVERYONE. No, haven't seen him, not yet, etc.

LOU. (*Going to office door.*) Vinnie, the "Vinnie Bumpcuss Stars of Tomorrow" are all here. You got something to say to them? I guess he's on the phone or something. It won't be much longer. The place is beginning to fill up. We already got the entire front row full of guys in trench coats. (*Exits.*)

BAMBY. My fan club! They always wear trench coats.

ROXIE. (*Imitating a flasher.*) ... and socks.

BAMBY. Well, Miss Corral, at least I got fans.

ROXIE. It's barn, Roxie Barn.

BAMBY. Excuse me, I knew it had something to do with farm animals.

LOTTA. (*Singing.*) "Old MacDonald had a farm, E I E I..."

HAL. O ... we've heard enough, Wendell and I are going outside to look for our friends. If Vinnie shows, let me know, we'll be outside in the alley. (*HAL exits, leaving his case behind.*)

SOMNAMBULO. Yes, a serious artist can't even think around here, let alone prepare for a performance. I must have silence! (*HE starts to go off to the bathroom.*)

ROXIE. (*Confronting Somnambulo.*) Hold it right there. Don't I know you from somewhere? ... Didn't we work together?

SOMNAMBULO. Who or what are you?

ROXIE. Roxie Barn, comedienne

SOMNAMBULO. No doubt the one they had in mind when the said "Comedy isn't pretty."

ROXIE. Now I remember you. You used to own a club across the state line, didn't you? ... It was a real pit ... the Do Drop Inn. I worked there when I was just starting out. It was ages ago ... (*Looking closely at his face.*) Say, who's your plastic surgeon, I can't even see the stitches.

SOMNAMBULO. You must have me confused with someone else, I would never appear in a pit. Now if you will excuse me I must prepare. (*HE exits into WC.*) And I must have silence!

(LOTTA sings a line from a song appropriate to the moment.)

ROXIE. I could have sworn that was the same guy ... Speaking of silence, I better go out front and check my mike before one of the "girls" here gets the bright idea to sabotage *my* act. (*Exits.*)
LOTTA. (*To Ian and Bamby.*) Well, you both know what I do, what's your claim to fame? (*SHE sings a line from a song appropriate to the moment.*)
BAMBY. Well, I'm a baton act, but I juggle and dance and my end lights up, it's like real patriotic, like you want to see?
LOTTA. The idea makes me very tired ... I mean your wrists need a west.
BAMBY. What?
LOTTA. West your wrists, they're weary.
BAMBY. Huh?
LOTTA. Never mind.
IAN. Well, I'm the trained dog act. Well, me and Fifi. We're called "La Cage aux Fifi," I thought of that myself. You see, one day I was giving Fifi her comb-out, singing along to Streisand, when I discovered Fifi could lip sync too, in fact she was a natural, so I tried her with Bette Midler, Beverly Sills, Liza and Diana Ross. It was a miracle! Fifi's lips actually moved right along with Diana's. She was supreme! Fifi is a born lip syncer with real star quality. Better than I ever was. That's when I realized that this was to be my calling in life. No sacrifice was too great! I quit cosmetology school! And devoted myself to Fifi, period. I knew then that I was destined to be

the mentor, manager and confidante of the world's greatest lip-syncing dog act.

SOMNAMBULO. (*From WC.*) I hate lip-syncing, I must have silence. (*FLUSH sound.*) Down, down, you're going down, spinning, spinning, going down. (*Opens bathroom door and enters in his turban and cape.*) Just rehearsing my act.

IAN. Anyway, back to the real talent. Oh, I know Fifi would just love to show you her act, if she could. Her big finish is really to die, it's our very own interpretation of TOTO. (*Pause.*) You know (*Pause.*) the dog from *The Wizard of Oz.* I wear the most fabulous red stiletto heels while Fifi lip syncs to "Somewhere over the Rainbow"... It's a guaranteed crowd pleaser, a real moment. I always cry.

BAMBY. (*Looking into the beer case.*) I'm sure she'll be fine for the show ... You've got me so excited, I really wish I could see some of it.

IAN. You know I could do just a few of the highlights. (*IAN does a part of the act with big finish.*)

LOTTA. (*Sings a line from a song appropriate to the moment.*) You should open the show tonight.

SOMNAMBULO. Open! He shouldn't be in the show. They both should go to the pound. I am an artist, and I am not following any lip-syncing dog in drag.

IAN. Fifi's not in drag. I am.

SOMNAMBULO. Have you no dignity?

BAMBY. Oh, I forgot. I better go potty before the contest or I might not be able to do my splits so good. (*Starts to open WC door and stops.*) Could someone turn the knob for me? My wrists still hurt.

LOTTA. (*Opening door for Bamby.*) So much for dignity. If you need help getting out ... (*SHE sings a line from a song appropriate to the moment.*)

IAN. This is in our act!

(*HAL enters during song.*
LOTTA continues to sing another line from a song appropriate to the moment.
IAN joins in.)

LOTTA. (*Grabbing Ian by the shirt and losing accent.*) Listen, buddy, I am the singer, you're the dog's assistant. (*Letting him go.*) Is that clear? [queer]

IAN. Well!

LOTTA (*To Somnambulo.*) What makes your act such a work of art, Swami?

SOMNAMBULO. I, madame, am a highly gifted and exceptionally trained hypnotist. I have even been a stand-by guest on the Pat Sajak show. Who amongst you can say the same?

BAMBY. Pat Sajak! Oooh, I had a dream about him once. (*FLUSH. Enters from WC.*) I bought a vowel.

SOMNAMBULO. To proceed. First, I select a member of the audience who looks to be weak-willed, I mean, a willing participant, and I place them in a deep hypnotic trance. Then I make them do things that they wouldn't normally do. Here, allow me to demonstrate. (*To Ian.*) You look like an excellent subject, my good fellow. Don't be afraid, it's all in harmless good fun.

IAN. I don't think so. You'll never be able to hypnotize me. I'm very strong-willed, and I never do foolish things.

SOMNAMBULO. *(Taking Ian by the face.)* Look into my eyes …

(IAN immediately falls into a trance.)

SOMNAMBULO. You are getting very sleepy. The sound of my voice is making you drowsy, you're going down, down, spinning. Are you feeling drowsy?

(LOTTA sings a line from a song appropriate to the moment.)

SOMNAMBULO. Can you hear me?
IAN. Yes, I can hear you!
SOMNAMBULO. How do you feel?
IAN. I feel all light and floaty, I feel like I'm flying … I feel like Doris Day in *Pillow Talk*. I feel like Billie Burke in everything she's ever done. I feel like Natalie Wood in *West Side Story*. *(HE sings a line from a song appropriate to the moment.)*
ROXIE. *(Entering from club and crossing to WC.)* Well, she's certainly witty and gay. *(SHE exits into WC.)*
SOMNAMBULO. Come in for a landing, Natalie, and stand still. Good, now when you hear the sound of a bell ringing you will think that you are …
BAMBY. Carmen Miranda. Make him into Carmen Miranda.
SOMNAMBULO. All right, *(Taking a small bell from his pocket.)* remember when you hear the sound of a bell ringing you will think you are Carmen Miranda. *(HE rings the bell.)*

(IAN immediately goes into an elaborate Carmen Miranda imitation.)

ROXIE. (*Entering from WC.*) What the hell is going on? What's this, Tammy Goes to Rio?

BAMBY. Be quiet, The Great Somnambulo hypnotized Ian and made him think he's Carmen Miranda. Isn't he sensational?

ROXIE. BFD! Fruit loops here already thinks he's Carmen Miranda. How about a real challenge. Why not make him macho?

SOMNAMBULO. There's a skeptic in every audience. All right! (*Taking Ian's face in his hand.*) Look into my eyes. You are no longer Carmen Miranda. When you hear the bell ring you will think that you are ... John Wayne. Do you hear me? When you hear the bell ring you will think you are "The Duke." (*HE rings bell.*)

IAN. (*Changes into John Wayne and grabs Roxie.*) OK, round 'em up, Pilgrim, you're in for it this time. I've put up with just about as much out of you as I aim to, one false move and you'll be singing with the angels. (*HE pins a terrified Roxie against the wall.*)

SOMNAMBULO. Satisfied?... When I snap my fingers you will no longer be John Wayne. Do you hear me?

IAN. I hear ya, Pilgrim?

SOMNAMBULO. When I snap my fingers you will be your old dizzy, swishy self.

IAN. (*Grabbing Somnambulo by the neck.*) Who you callin' swishy, Pilgrim!?

SOMNAMBULO. (*Panicked.*) One ... Two ... Three. (*Snap.*)

IAN. (*Back to himself.*) See, I told you I couldn't be hypnotized. Better luck with the audience tonight.

BAMBY. Oh, but Ian, he did hypnotize you. It was incredible.

IAN. He did?... Oh God, was I embarrassing?

ROXIE. No more than usual.

LOTTA He made you think you were John Wayne.

IAN. John Wayne!

LOTTA You were so strong and daring and virile. [vy-will]

ROXIE. What?

LOTTA. Virile. [vy-will]

ROXIE. Huh?

LOTTA/BAMBY. Never mind.

BAMBY. You were a real man's man.

IAN. I was? Did anyone get my phone number? Oh, I'm all flushed. I better go freshen up. Anyone have a "Wet One"? (*Exits into WC.*)

HAL. Wendell and I do a mind-reading act that's as good as that. Someone help me blindfold Wendell?

(*LOTTA uses her long scarf to blindfold Wendell and we see a blood stain on her scarf.*)

HAL. Now if someone in the room will hold up an object "The Amazing Wendell" will be able to describe it to you.

BAMBY. (*Pulls out a glitzy bra from her bag.*) I have something, I have something, let me do it.

HAL. Tell us what you see, Wendell.

WENDELL. It's very dark.

HAL. Now Wendell, concentrate, look into the astral plane.

WENDELL. Wait, I'm getting something, it's something to do with dinnerware ... it's plates ... no, no ... it's bowls, no, no ... it's cups ... two cups ... two D cups ... it's a lady's bra.

BAMBY. That's amazing! How does he do that?

SOMNAMBULO. There's more than one dummy in this room.

(The wall PHONE rings.
IAN goes into Carmen Miranda act.
SOMNAMBULO snaps fingers at Ian to stop Carmen.)

BAMBY. (*After second ring.*) Oh, I'll get it, it's probably for me, one of my fans. (*Answers phone.*) Hello ... yes this is the Belly Laugh although there aren't too many around here right now. Oh yeah, she's here, hold on ... (*To Roxie.*) it's for you ... (*Drops phone.*) I think I better go check to see where I can get some power. Lou! Can you tell where I can plug it in? (*BAMBY exits the club with an extension cord.*)

LOU. Anytime, baby, anytime. (*Follows her out.*)

ROXIE. (*Into phone, speaking softly.*) Yeah ... I told you not to never to call me.

(Rest of the CAST stops and listens.)

ROXIE. Do you mind?

(THEY all look away.)

ROXIE. No it won't start for a few more minutes ... I told you ... it'll all be fine after tonight ... I'm not going to miss my chance this time ... no, a gun would be too loud... Don't worry. It should all be over in an hour ... I'll see you later. Then we can really celebrate.

(The LIGHTS go out, EVERYONE screams, much hubub. LIGHTS are restored to reveal a variety of situations.)

IAN. *(Standing at the office door with pants down and a nail file trying to pry open the office door.)* Hello, hello ...

(WC door opens and EVERYONE else is in the bathroom.)

LOU. *(Entering in a rush.)* OK, the power's back on, but me and the little lady think someone's been tampering with her act and tried to electrocute her. That's why the fuse blew. You OK, honey?
BAMBY. *(Enters looking like a fried chicken.)* I feel a little bit funny but I think I'll be OK if I can just have a drink of water.
LOU. I want to make sure this doesn't happen again. Everyone better go out front and check their stuff before the show begins. *(With his arm around Bamby.)* We wouldn't want to damage this little bundle of talent.

(LOTTA sings a line from a song appropriate to the moment.)

EVERYONE. SHUT UP!
LOTTA. Sorry!

(SOMNAMBULO realizes he has left his turban on the sofa, goes back to get it, picks it up and a folded piece of paper falls out. HE grabs it up and tries to hide it from view.

After the stage is empty IAN peeks around the door of the washroom and quietly slips out. Seeing that he is alone HE starts to go through Bamby's things. HE pulls out the skimpy glitzy bra and holds it up, imagining himself in it. Digging deeper HE pulls out a large jewel-studded dagger with a long blade. HE starts posing with her things when HE hears SOMEONE coming from the outside. HE drops the things back into the bag and ducks down and hides. HAL enters from the alley. Looking around to make sure the cost is clear, HE goes to the phone, puts in a coin and dials a number.)

HAL. (*Into the phone.*) This is the "dummy" calling. Everything is about to start. Where are the "friends"?… Great, he won't get away from us tonight. This time the chickens come home to roost and we'll be waiting for them. (*HE hangs up, checking to see that he's still alone HE takes out his gun and checks it to make sure it's loaded. IAN watching and hearing all of this from his hiding place, is wide-eyed with terror.*)

BAMBY. (*Offstage.*) Ian! Ian, you need to come set up your act.

(Both IAN and HAL jump at the sound of Bamby's voice. THEY see each other. HAL starts advancing towards Ian with the gun drawn, IAN grabs the beer case with the still sleepy Fifi inside. HE holds it up in front him.)

IAN. Don't shoot! Don't shoot! We didn't hear anything, Mr. Dummy sir. I didn't see your gun or anything, did we, Fifi? Don't shoot, I can't stand the sight of blood, especially mine.

HAL. Put the dog down and everything will be ...

BAMBY. (*Entering from club.*) Ian, didn't you hear me? You need to come check Fifi's props. Oh, good you got Fifi up. You better get in there now the show is going to start.

(*HAL has turned away and shoved his gun back into his
    coat.*)

IAN. I'm off like a bullet! I mean a shot. Come on, Fifi, our public awaits. (*With the beer case under his arm HE dashes out as LOU comes in, followed by the rest of the CAST.*)

LOU. As soon as Lassie comes home we can start. Now, I know that you are all a bit jittery so as soon as Vinnie gives you his spiel we can get this carnival on the road. (*HE goes to Vinnie's door, and KNOCKS.*) Vinnie, whatever you're up to, it will have to wait. The show's got to go on ... Vinnie, you in there? ... (*No answer.*) VINNIE ... (*LOU opens the door to reveal VINNIE standing there with a shocked expression on his face.*) ... Oh, Vinnie, great, you're still here. These are the finalists in the "Vinnie Bumpcuss Talent Search." Everybody, this is Vinnie Bumpcuss.

(*On that, VINNIE falls face forward onto the floor with a
    knife sticking out of his back.*

*EVERYONE screams, chaos ensues. LOU and HAL catch
Vinnie before he hits the floor. His toupee flies off and
BAMBY catches it.)*

SOMNAMBULO. Ye gods, he's been stabbed.
BAMBY. (*With toupee in hand.*) He's been scalped!
LOTTA. He looks very tired.

*(HAL takes a close look at the body. EVERYONE is now
frozen in shock.)*

HAL. He's more than tired, Miss Verboten, he's dead.
IAN. (*Enters talking to Fifi.*) Is my little Fifi feeling
better now? You don't have a hangover, do you? (*IAN sees
everyone looking down at the floor. HE looks down and
shrieks.*) Oh my God! Don't look, Fifi! Don't look.
(*Pointing at HAL who is still kneeling beside the body.*)
Murderer! Murderer!

(EVERYONE turns back to look at Hal.)

IAN. He's got a gun, I saw it.

(THEY all start to move away from Hal.)

HAL. (*Standing up and pulling out his gun.*) Hold it!
Hands up, everybody stay right where you are, nobody
move.

(ALL flee to opposite wall.)

IAN. I told you, he means to gun us all down.

HAL. Relax, I'm not the murderer and I'm not a ventriloquist.

BAMBY. You're not? He sure fooled me.

HAL. I'm Detective Howard Brown of the Police Vice Squad. (*HE holds up his badge.*) Now just calm down and everything will be all right.

ROXIE. I knew he wasn't a ventriloquist from the first time I saw his lips move.

LOU. What's a vice cop like you doing in a dump like this?

HAL. We've had this place under surveillance for weeks now. (*To Lou.*) Your boss, the late Mr. Bumpcuss, had a great little racket going, didn't he, running the numbers outta his club?

LOU. Hey, I'm just the MC, I don't know nothing about it.

ROXIE. Me either. I hardly knew the guy.

BAMBY. He ain't even my type.

(*ALL look at Ian.*)

IAN. With a toupee? Not on your life.

HAL. Well he was someone's type. Someone right here in this room.

LOTTA. What do you mean, officer? You don't think one of us killed this man?

HAL. Not think it, Miss Verboten, I know it. I got here before anyone but Lou. Remember, Lou? I was hiding in the washroom when I heard you telling Vinnie that if he didn't have the dough tonight there was going to be trouble. Am I right, Lou?

LOU. Yeah, I remember something like that.

HAL. Was he going to scram with the loot and leave you holding the bag?

LOU. No, I swear, Vinnie was like a brother to me. I didn't do nothing.

HAL. Well if not you, then one of these characters had to have done it. Since I've arrived this place has been surrounded. I've got eight guys in trench coats out in the club since it opened.

ROXIE. Oh, yeah, so much for Miss Sniff and Twirls fan club.

(BAMBY sniffs and turns.)

HAL. I've been here and out in the alley, both entrances were covered before the five of you arrived. And no one else has gone in or out.

LOTTA. If any one of us could have done it, how are you going to prove which one of us it is?

EVERYONE. Yeah!

HAL. Simple, witnesses.

ROXIE. Witnesses, my ass. Where you going to get witnesses if it's just us five and all of us was out of the room at one time or another? Where's your witnesses?

HAL. Oh, we got witnesses *(Pointing out at the audience.)* and they've seen everything you've done here tonight. OK, boys, bring up the lights.

(The HOUSE LIGHTS come up. The CAST lets out a yell in frightened disbelief, with much ad-libbing and trying not to look embarrassed.)

HAL. So while we remove the body and send down to the lab for some tests, why don't we take a little break? Right now I need some volunteers to help me chalk out the crime scene and get rid of the body.

(CAST looks relieved and starts to move off.)

HAL. Wait right there! You're not going anywhere. These good people are going to keep an eye on you to make sure you don't try to escape, and while they're at it they might just have a few questions to ask you about your activities this evening. *(To the audience.)* We'll be right back. Don't be shy, this is your chance to find out the facts.

(The CAST [in character] go into the audience and try to convince them that they are innocent. HAL and TWO VOLUNTEERS chalk out Vinnie's outline on the floor and help remove the body.)

End of ACT I

ACT II

The HOUSE LIGHTS are still up. The CAST have returned and are scattered among the audience.

HAL. (*Entering from offstage.*) Would all of the suspects please return to the crime scene? (*HE calls out each name, and one-by-one forces THEM to come up on stage.*) Ok, everyone, I've just received word from headquarters, no one can leave unless I say so. (*To cast.*) You're all prime suspects, (*To audience.*) and you're all material witnesses. (*Picking up male AUDIENCE MEMBER.*) Sir, you have an honest face, would you please assist me? Take this and tie the end of it over there. (*HE hands the end of the police "crime scene" tape to AUDIENCE MEMBER. THEY rope off the seating area.*) Now, no one goes in or out until we've gathered all the evidence. While we're waiting for the lab to call with the test results, I would like you all to stand up. Raise your right hand and repeat after me. (*Oath.*) I, STATE YOUR NAME ... DO SOLEMNLY SWEAR ... THAT AS A MATERIAL WITNESS TO THIS SENSELESS CRIME ... I WILL NEVER REVEAL THE IDENTITY OF VINNIE'S MURDERER ... AS DETERMINED BY TONIGHT'S INVESTIGATION ... IF I BREAK THIS OATH ... I AGREE TO SPEND A WEEK ON A DESERT ISLAND ... WITH IAN, BAMBY AND FIFI ... Good, you may sit down. Now, I want you all to think back and try to remember anything that seemed suspicious.

All we know for sure is that Vinnie was stabbed in the back with a knife, and any one of you could have done it.

SOMNAMBULO. A knife! Isn't that typically a woman's weapon?

(MEN and WOMEN separate, IAN is left in the middle. IAN has to choose which side to go with, thinks for a second and becomes very butch and goes over to the men's side.)

HAL. I'm in charge of this investigation, Mr. Somnambulo, and I'll draw the conclusions. Now, you, Miss Barn, you were the first of the contestants to arrive, and at the time you seemed more than a little surprised to see anyone here.

ROXIE. So what? Since when is it a crime to come early? And why me? I'm a comedienne. The only thing I try to do is kill 'em with laughs. Besides, Vinnie's office door was locked, and none of us went in there tonight.

SOMNAMBULO. She's right, Kojak. Even the great Somnambulo couldn't slip through a key hole to kill him, not that I would have. So explain that.

HAL. I will. No one did go through that door to kill Vinnie, but there's another way in. There's a door in the john that open directly into the office. Anyone of you could have slipped in and committed the murder, and if I'm not mistaken all of you were alone in there long enough to do it. And one of you did.

LOU. Yeah, but that door's been locked for years. I don't even think Vinnie had a key.

HAL. Ah, but that's where you're wrong, Mr. Dumbello. Miss Barn, if you would bring me your coat from the hook.

ROXIE. (*Takes coat off hook, brings it to Hal.*) This doesn't go with the rest of your outfit. (*SHE holds up coat.*)

HAL. (*Picking older female AUDIENCE MEMBER.*) Now, madame, would you please assist me? Go through the pockets of her coat and tell us what you find.

(*AUDIENCE MEMBER pulls out cupcakes, Fritos and a condom.*)

HAL. What is that?

(*WOMAN is forced to read or say condom.*)

ROXIE. You never know, a girl could get lucky.

IAN. Well, I hope you brought enough for everyone.

HAL. (*Turning coat to other pocket.*) Would you please look in this pocket, madame?

(*WOMAN pulls out a key on a ring.*)

HAL. What is that, madame?

WOMAN. A key!

HAL. A key!

CAST. A KEY!

ROXIE. A KEY! Big deal, what is this, Spanish lessons? I never saw that key before in my life.

HAL. (*Takes the key and the coat.*) Excellent work, you should be on the vice squad. (*Giving her a badge.*) You are now an official Knock 'em Dead dick. Please give this lovely lady a hand for her help.

ROXIE. I'm telling ya, I never saw that key before.

HAL. (*Holding up the key.*) Perhaps, Miss Barn, but watch and learn. Now if you will all observe. (*HAL goes through the door between the two rooms and opens Vinnie's office door and stand there.*) You see how easy murder can be.

ROXIE. That key's not mine. I don't know who put it in my pocket.

HAL. Any one of you could have made a wax impression of that lock when you were here the last time you competed. Then it would be a simple matter to have a key made that opened the lock and use it tonight to get at Vinnie. Including you, Mr. Dumbello.

ROXIE. Someone is trying to frame me. I'm telling you, if I find out who it was there will be hell to pay.

HAL. Exactly. Someone will pay. Before the night's over we'll establish the owner of the key and reveal the identity of Vinnie's murderer.

LOU. That's great! While we sit here playing twenty questions, I got a club full of rowdy patrons who paid good money to see a talent show. If we don't give 'em some entertainment, no matter how crummy it is, they're gonna tear the place down. So we ain't got time for games.

BAMBY. Oh, I love games. I'm real good at spin-the-bottle.

LOTTA. The only game I'm good at is "Name That Tune." Let's get on with the show. I came to win this stinking contest. I need the thousand bucks.

SOMNAMBULO. Yes, we must go forward. You, sir, are not of the theatre. We do not allow something as trivial as murder to stop us. The show must go on, as a tribute to Vinnie.

LOU. Yeah, Vinnie would have wanted it that way.

IAN, BAMBY, ROXIE. (*ALL are becoming rowdy.*) Yeah, I need the cash, I came to win, etc. etc.

HAL. Calm down! Calm down! No problem. You can go on with the contest if it will keep you cool. Just remember those eight guys in trench coats I got out front. No one's getting out that way unless they want to be carried out.

IAN. I just hope Fifi's nerve aren't affected by this awful tragedy.

BAMBY. I don't get it. How will the contest work without Vinnie?

HAL. Lou will introduce you like he always does, you'll do your act, then come right back. Meanwhile the interrogation will continue.

LOTTA. Well, who goes on first?

ROXIE. You already tried to pin the rap on me. Let me go out there and get it over with. I don't know about the rest of you, but I could use a few laughs.

LOU. Looks like you're the first victim. (*LOU and ROXIE start to exit.*) Except for Vinnie. He's running that big comedy club in the sky.

HAL. Just remember I've got a few more questions for you, Miss Barn.

ROXIE. (*Exiting.*) Yeah, while you're at it, why not question the bimbo, she's too dumb to be real.

BAMBY. ME? How could anyone suspect me? I'm injured, remember my wrists. There's no way I could have stabbed him.

HAL. (*Directing Bamby to the chair under the light.*)
Let's talk about that, Miss Lynn.

(*AUDIENCE questions Bamby.*
At the end of questions:)

HAL. Well, I'm glad you were able to get that off your
chest, Miss Bamby.
LOU. (*Returning with ROXIE.*) You're up next,
Bamby. After her act, they'll go crazy for you. Show 'em
what you got.
BAMBY. (*Holding wrists like they still hurt.*) I never
hide my assets, I'll do the best I can. Lou, could you get
my bag? My public awaits.
LOU. Sure thing, gorgeous. (*THEY exit into club.*)
ROXIE. (*Entering.*) I knocked 'em dead out there, I
mean I killed them, I slayed them. I mean ... I don't mean
... I didn't do it.
HAL. So you say, Miss Barn. Now just take a seat and
I'll get to you in a minute. (*Turns to Ian.*) But right now I
want to ask Ian a few questions.
IAN. (*Rising from chair.*) Well, I didn't want to say
anything while she was in the room, but guess what I
found in *her* bag? ... A knife, this long.
HAL. Yes, I remember seeing that knife in *your* hands.
I think you better sit here and tell us about it.

(*AUDIENCE questions Ian.*
At end of questions:)

HAL. Well, no one saw what happened in the dark, but before the night's over we'll shed some light on the whole situation.

ROXIE. I think you're questioning the wrong person. One of us is not who they claim to be. (*Looking at Somnambulo.*) Are they? He's a fake and I know it.

SOMNAMBULO. (*Indignant.*) I've had just about enough of these insults. I'm leaving! (*Starts to exit through audience.*)

HAL. Stop that man!

LOU. (*Coming on.*) I've got him, give me a hand. He's not going anywhere. (*Brings SOMNAMBULO back on stage. To Lotta.*) Bamby's batons are burning, she's almost to her climax. Lotta, I guess you're up next. I'll introduce you.

LOTTA. Don't bother, some artists need no introduction. (*SHE exits singing.*)

HAL. (*To Somnambulo, in chair.*) You were awfully eager to leave us, weren't you, Mr. Great?

SOMNAMBULO. This is absurd, this is a travesty.

ROXIE. Travesty is right! He's a sham! He's a fake! And we both know it. Ask him about that dive, the DO DROP INN.

HAL. Thank you, Miss Barn. Did any of you see this man do anything suspicious?

(*AUDIENCE questions Somnambulo.
At end of questions:*)

HAL. You seem to have something to hide, Mr. Great.

SOMNAMBULO. I have nothing to hide, you can't prove a thing. And stop calling me Mr. Great.

ROXIE. OK, Mr. Mediocre.

BAMBY. (*Entering.*) They loved me. I was worried about my wrists, but those guys in the trench coats went wild when I did my high kicks.

ROXIE. Sure they did, they're used to legs in the air. They're the vice squad.

BAMBY. Fans are fans. Too bad the pig breeders aren't here for you, Miss Barn.

HAL. Hold it, ladies, we've heard about enough from you. (*To Somnambulo.*) I know you're lying but ...

SOMNAMBULO. (*Moving from chair.*) I'm always suspicious of those who are over-eager to lay the blame on someone else. As we say in the world of opera, it ain't over until the FAT lady sings. What about that phone call she got? (*Indicating Roxie.*)

HAL. Yes, tell us about it, Miss Barn.

LOTTA. (*Entering.*) Pigs, pearls before swine, they wouldn't know great art if it reached up and bit them on the ass.

LOU. In that case they're going to love the princess and the pooch. Come on, Cinderella, you're next.

IAN. (*Grabbing the dog and the rest of his props.*) This is it, Fifi, now's our big chance. Eat your heart out, Cher, here comes Fifi. (*HE exits with LOU.*)

HAL. There's something really strange about that man. Now, everyone's here who was involved in that suspicious phone call to Miss Barn.

(*AUDIENCE questions Roxie.*
At end of questions:)

HAL. Aha, that phone call certainly did sound suspicious to me, Miss Barn.

ROXIE. (*Indicating Lotta.*) If anything sounds suspicious, it's that Marlene Dietrich meets Elmer Fudd accent she's been faking all night.

LOTTA. There's nothing fake about me, I'm the only really genuine article here and these good people know it. (*SHE goes into audience and sits on a man's lap.*) You believe me darling, don't you?

IAN. (*Entering weeping, with Fifi in his arms.*) How could anybody boo the *Wizard of Oz*? (*Turns back and yells.*) Barbarians! That's what you are, barbarians. Oh, Auntie Em, there's no place like home, there's no place like home. (*Collapses in tears.*)

LOU. Hey, you with the turban, you're bringing up the rear.

SOMNAMBULO. It's fortunate that they saved the best for last. Somnambulo always satisfies. Make way for the winner.

LOTTA. (*Still sitting on man's lap.*) Let me put my head on your shoulder.

HAL. This is no time for a nap, Miss Verboten. Now exactly what was the name of that club you played in Toledo?

(*AUDIENCE questions Lotta.*
At end of questions:)

HAL. It all seems a little off-key to me, Miss Verboten, if that's really your name. But before the night's over someone here will be crooning the blues and headed for Sing Sing.

LOU. (*Entering.*) Well, he's really putting them to sleep out there. Half the audience is snoring. At least he's the last of them. Solved it yet, copper? You want to know who I suspect …

HAL. Not right now, Mr. Dumbello. But I think we've got a few questions for you, have a seat.

LOU. Me? Vinnie was my best friend, my pal. I got no reason to kill him.

HAL. Maybe not, but what about your career? Why didn't Vinnie let you perform? And what about that phone call you tried to make, who were you calling?

LOU. When Vinnie's door was locked so long, I called his number to see if he was in there. It was busy, big deal, that's the ONLY call I made.

HAL. (*To audience.*) Is that so? We know you made a second call, and it was this number written right here. (*Indicates number on wall.*) Maybe we should just try it now and see who answers. (*HE goes to audience.*) Has anyone got a quarter? (*HE keeps it up until HE gets one or more quarters.*)

LOU. No, don't bother, it's my wife Rosalie's car phone. I wanted to check on where she was. I never got her, it was busy. She's always out running around.

HAL. OK, I'll buy it for now. It's easy enough to check the number. (*HE pockets the quarters.*) I'll just keep this quarter in case I need it. It seems to me, Lou, that you had the most to gain and the least to lose from Vinnie's death. Anybody got a question for Mr. Dumbello?

(*AUDIENCE questions Lou.*
At end of questions:)

LOU. In this country it takes more than suspicion to send somebody up the river.

LOTTA. (*Singing.*) God bless America.

SOMNAMBULO. (*Entering from club.*) I was a triumph! They were extraordinarily attentive. You could have heard a pin drop in that room.

ROXIE. Cut the crap. Lou already told us, you bored 'em to tears and they fell asleep. If you could bottle your act you could put Sominex out of business.

HAL. We've heard enough from you, in fact we've heard just about enough from everybody.

LOU. We haven't heard from that mob out there. I've got to go out there, wake them up and see which of these losers deserves to win. (*HE exits.*)

HAL. While he's out there counting votes for the winner, we'll be in here counting votes to finger the killer. Now I need two volunteers from the audience to help. (*HE brings TWO PEOPLE up on stage and gives each a note pad and pencil.*) What's your name? (*THEY answer.*) Fine, you are now officially Deputy _____________ and Deputy ________________. (*To audience.*) It's time for the witnesses to weigh the facts. You've seen the evidence and you've heard their alibis. Now it's all up to you. As I name each suspect, please raise your hand for the one you think killed Vinnie. My deputies and I will count the votes that determine the murderer.

(*As each is named THEY continue to protest their innocence.*)

HAL. (*Going to each suspect.*) Was it Miss Verboten? The chanteuse with the questionable accent.

Is is The Great Somnambulo? Even his turban can't hide his secret past.

Is Bamby Lynn the one? The baton twirler with the miraculously healing wrists.

Is it Ian and Fifi? Always eager to point their limp-wristed paw at someone else.

Or Roxie Barn? The loud mouth who quiets down for her fishy phone call.

LOU. (*Entering in a hurry.*) The voting is almost over, I'll be back in a flash with the winner's name.

HAL. (*Indicating Lou.*) Or last but not least, Lou Dumbello, the greasy MC who knew Vinnie well, maybe too well? In a few moments we'll know the truth and one of them will end up behind bars. Can I have the vote count, deputies?

(THEY give Hal the tabulation and HE thanks them.)

HAL. Well the verdict is in. (*Holding up the tally.*) And it's just as I suspected … (*The PHONE rings.*) Don't move I'll get it.

(IAN goes into his Carmen Miranda imitation, while HAL goes to phone.
ALL snap their fingers to bring IAN out of it.)

HAL. Hello, yeah, this is Brown … Is that so? That's a very interesting turn of events. Oddly enough, with the help of my witnesses here, we've come to the same conclusion. Call me when you get the final results, I'll handle it at this end. (*HE hangs up and turns slowly to the cast.*)

BAMBY. What did they say?

IAN. Was that the lab?

LOTTA. Don't keep us in suspense.

HAL. It seems like Vinnie left us a clue. When they got him to the morgue they found clenched in his hand a scrap of paper.

****
GO TO MURDER INSERTS
****

IAN. (*As John Wayne.*) It's the last roundup, Pilgrim.

(*MURDERER turns in surprise.
IAN grabs the gun, grapples with Murderer.*)

HAL. Get 'em, Duke. (*Gun drops to floor, HAL grabs it.*) Looks like the jig's up for good, [Murderer's name.] (*Takes Murderer from Ian.*) Thanks, Duke. The good guys win again.

(*MURDERER has fallen to the floor.*)

IAN. (*Back to self, drops to floor terrified.*) We're going to die, Fifi. We're all going to die (*Looks at Murderer.*) What happened?

ROXIE. She/He's fallen and can't get up.

HAL. You saved the day, John Wayne returned, you saved the day.

IAN. Remember the Alamo.

HAL. Come on. (*Handcuffing murderer.*) I'm putting you behind bars, right where you belong.

LOU. Wait! That's the winner. You've arrested the Head Chuckle. What about the thousand bucks? What about the contract?

MURDERER. Great! I can use the money to pay for my defense.

HAL. We got an iron clad contract for you. Twenty years to life at the state pen

LOTTA. He/She may be the murderer, but only because he/she got there first. I came here tonight to kill Vinnie. He was a rat. He was scum. He was my father.

EVERYONE. Your father???!!

LOTTA. Yes. Vinnie was my father. I'm ashamed to admit it. He deserted my mother and us kids when I was just a baby. He took everything, and left us destitute. We were put in an institute. Mama became a prostitute and died from a broken heart. I was raised by nuns at "Our Lady of Spain convent." I never saw my brother and sister again. I swore then if I ever had the chance I would make him pay for what he did to us. It took years but I finally tracked him down to this little corner of hell. All I ever had to keep me going was this lock of my mother's hair (*SHE pulls out pendant on a chain.*) You can rest now, Mama, it's all over you've been avenged.

IAN. A locket! You mean like this one? (*Pulls out identical locket.*)

BAMBY. Wait a minute, I've got one of those too. (*SHE pulls out locket.*)

IAN. (*To Lotta.*) SISTER! (*To Bamby.*) SISTER!

LOTTA & BAMBY. (*To Ian, after a moment of hesitation.*) SISTER?

ALL THREE. (*Look at lockets, then up to heaven.*) OH, MAMA!

ROXIE. OH, brother.

HAL. (*To Murderer.*) Family reunion or not, you're headed for the slammer.

MURDERER. (*As THEY exit.*) Just my luck, for once I have a shot at the big time and I end up in jail.

HAL. Well you know what they say …

ALL. That's SHOW-BIZ

BLACKOUT

THE END

MURDERER INSERTS

"A" ROXIE
"B" IAN
"C" SOMNAMBULO
"D" LOTTA
"E" LOU
"F" BAMBY

MURDERER "A"

ROXIE

HAL. A piece of green paper with the letters R-R written on it

IAN. Ronald Reagan did it?

SOMNAMBULO. That clears me, those aren't my initials.

HAL. Someone in this room used to have those initials ... (*Turning to Roxie.*) didn't they Miss Barn, or should I say "Rocky." (*Pulling his gun from his coat.*)

ROXIE. Initials, big deal. Where's the proof?

HAL. The proof is on the paper, along with your thumb print. After that it was easy to establish your true identity "Rocky Road."

ALL. ROCKY ROAD!

ROXIE. Yes, you're right, I used to be Rocky Road. Life was different then, I was a hot young comic, the Carson Show, Vegas, I had it all. You know the rest, the tragic accident, the scandal, it was all over the tabloids, I was ruined ...

LOU. (*Running in.*) I got the winner, I got the winner. You'll never guess who won, I couldn't believe it myself, I had to recount ...

(*Interruption by Lou causes HAL's distraction. Struggle ensues, ROXIE gets gun from Lou. EVERYONE screams and runs, IAN hides behind couch.*)

ROXIE. (*Now out of control.*) Sure, I did it, and I'd do it again. He had it coming, and I'll tell you why. After that night I didn't work for years, the media tore me to shreds. I went into hiding in Mexico. But it was no good. I was addicted to comedy, I had to get back on stage, any way, any how. There was only one way, no one would suspect that Rocky Road had become a woman. Now I could follow my show biz dream. It was all beginning to work again, playing the little clubs, all I needed was a thousand bucks to get my last hormone treatment, then it was back to the big time. That's why I entered this contest. Vinnie remembered my old material, recognized me and tried to blackmail me. This time nothing was going to stand in my way, I had to kill him, don't you understand I did it for laughs.

(*PHONE rings,*)

HAL. (*Answers.*) Send help!

(*IAN rises up as John Wayne.*)

ROXIE. Comedy's in my blood, I'll make it big again, no one is going to get in my way. Vinnie didn't and neither will any of you ...

BACK TO SCRIPT

IAN. It's the last roundup, Pilgrim ...

MURDERER "B"

IAN

HAL. A piece of pink paper with the letters G-O-D.

BAMBY. G O D. GOD! It was a miracle!

SOMNAMBULO. I've been known to perform miracles, but not this one. I'm in the clear.

HAL. Yes, but those letters implicate someone in this room. We've discovered that Vinnie was dyslexic and backwards G-O-D spells ... (*Turning to Ian.*) DOG isn't that right, Ian?

IAN. Big deal, C-A-T spells cat, where's the proof?

HAL. The proof is on the paper, along with your thumb print, after that it was easy. Under that prissy exterior hides the cold steel soul of a killer. You're headed for the big house and the pooch is headed for the pound.

IAN. Yes, you're right, but it was justice, Before I had Fifi, I had her mother, Zaza. She was so talented, so glamorous, she was destined to be a star. We were out for our evening stroll when a big black car came out of the twilight and hit poor little Zaza and sped away, but not before I got the license number.

LOU. (*Running in.*) I got a winner, I got a winner, you'll never guess who won, I can't believe it myself, I had to recount ...

(*Interruption by Lou causes HAL's momentary distraction.
A struggle ensues, IAN grabs the gun from Hal.
EVERYONE screams and runs.*)

IAN. (*Now holding the gun is mad with power and out of control.*) Yes, I did it, and I'd do it again. I was only the limp wrist of justice. It took me years to track down the driver of that killer car. All the while I was searching for the cold blooded murderer of Zaza, I was training her daughter, Fifi, to follow in her mother's paw steps. It was fate that the owner of the car, Vincent T. Bumpcuss, and Vinnie Bumpcuss of "Belly Laugh" fame were one and the same. I planned carefully, we rehearsed our tushes off to get our chance at revenging Zaza and tonight my planning paid off. I had to kill him, don't you see? I did it for poor orphaned Fifi.

(*PHONE rings, instantly IAN becomes Carmen Miranda. HAL grabs back the gun from Ian, taking control.*)

HAL. Looks like your dancing days are over Carmen. (*HE snaps fingers.*)
IAN. (*Back to himself.*) Oh God, Fifi what will become of us?

BACK TO SCRIPT

HAL. Come on, I'm putting you behind bars, right where you belong, etc., etc.

MURDERER "C"

SOMNAMBULO

HAL. A piece of gold paper with the letters Z Z written on it.

IAN. Zaza Gabor! Throw the book at her, she deserves it.

SOMNAMBULO. Well it certainly can't implicate me. Those aren't any of my initials, so if you'll please excuse me I'll be on ... (*HE starts to leave.*)

HAL. Not so fast. (*Stopping Somnambulo.*) What makes you think those are anyone's initials? I think Vinnie was trying to tell us somethin'.

SOMNAMBULO. Like what? Zazu Pitts did it? Where's your proof?

HAL. The proof is on the paper, along with a thumb print. It didn't take much to trace that thumb print to you, Mr.   . You used to own a club called the DO DROP INN didn't you? Along with a partner, a Mr. Vincent T. Bumpcuss. You're the one who killed Vinnie.

SOMNAMBULO. Yeah, I did it, he had it coming. All those years I worked to make that club into something. It was all I had. It meant the world to me. I was short of cash, I took in a business partner. Everything was going fine, then one day the cops busted in, the club was being used as a front for a gambling ring. My partner had taken it on the lam, taking all of our money and leaving me to take the rap for a crime I didn't commit.

LOU. *(Running in.)* I got a winner, I got a winner, you'll never guess who won! I can't believe it myself, I had to recount ...

(Lou's interruption causes HAL's momentary distraction. SOMNAMBULO grabs the gun from Hal, points at the others. EVERYONE screams and runs. IAN hides behind the sofa.)

SOMNAMBULO. *(Holding the gun and out of control.)* Do you blame me for doing it? For ten stinking years I rotted in the state prison, can you imagine me in prison? It was hell. But it gave me time, plenty of time to perfect my revenge and my skills at hypnotism. After I got out it was easy to track down my ex-partner, Mr. Vincent Bumpcuss. All I had to do was wait for the chance to get him alone. I saw the ad for this cheesy talent contest and I knew my chance had arrived. The rest was easy, just like you said. But you're not going to send me back to that stinking prison, I'm getting out of here ...

(PHONE rings, IAN raises up from behind sofa as John Wayne.)

SOMNAMBULO. Don't try any funny business, I'm getting out of here and if I have to I'll take one of you with me ...

BACK TO SCRIPT

MURDERER "D"

LOTTA

HAL. A piece of off-white paper with three letters scrawled on it, three letters he managed to write before he died. S-I-S

IAN. His sister did it?

HAL. Not *his* sister, Ian, *a* sister.

SOMNAMBULO. Well I'm an only child, guess that clears me.

HAL. So was Vinnie, and that's what had us confused at first. until I asked, When is a sister not a sister? Maybe you can tell us the answer to that, Sister Lisa Alleluia de Bologna. (*Looking at Lotta.*)

LOTTA. S-I-S-That's nothing. Maybe he couldn't spell S-O-S. Maybe he was trying to write sissy. (*Points at Ian. Back to Hal.*) Where's your proof?

HAL. The proof is on the paper, along with your thumb print, Sister. After that it was easy to establish your identity. Or do I have to call the OUR LADY OF SPAIN CONVENT?

ALL. The Convent!

LOTTA. (*Dropping accent completely.*) No, don't call the convent, I couldn't face the Abbess. I admit it. I did it, and I'm glad, glad, glad! You've heard of the singing nun, you've heard of the flying nun, well I'm Sister Lisa, the Ninja nun. (*SHE pulls off wig to reveal nun-like demeanor.*) The sisters taught me the difference between good and evil, and Vinnie was EVIL. He deserved to die.

When I became a nun, I vowed to track him down and get my revenge.

LOU. (*Enters.*) I got the winner, I got the winner. You'll never guess who won, I couldn't believe it myself, I had to recount ...

(*Interruption of Lou causes HAL to be distracted, LOTTA gets gun from Lou. ALL scream and hide, IAN behind couch.*)

LOTTA. Yes, I did it and I'd do it again. I came here tonight to kill Vinnie. He was a rat, he was scum, he was my father!
ALL. Your father!!??

(*PHONE rings, IAN goes into John Wayne.*)

LOTTA. Yes, my father. Daddy dumped my mother and me before I was born, but his lowlife genes made me thirsty for vengeance. I'm a bad seed.

(*IAN grabs Lotta.*)

BACK TO SCRIPT

IAN. It's the last roundup, Pilgrim ...

MURDERER "E"

LOU

HAL. A piece of paper with the letters H-E-L-L on it.

BAMBY. Hell? The devil did it?

SOMNAMBULO. Hell? That's obviously where he went.

LOU. (*Enters.*) I got the winner, I got the winner. You'll never guess who won, I couldn't believe it myself. I had to recount ...

HAL. (*Cutting Lou off.*) And I had to rethink. It took me a minute, Lou. What is H-E-L-L upside down?

LOU. Got me.

BAMBY. I know, I know. Hell upside down would be heaven ... the angels did it?

HAL. Wrong again, Bamby. H E L L turned upside down become numbers, don't they, Lou? The numbers 7764. Sound familiar?

LOU. Four numbers, big deal. What's that prove?

HAL. They prove plenty. Those four numbers just happen to be the last four digits of your wife Rosalie's car phone number. The number you tried desperately to reach, the same number written here on the wall, the number you lied about.

LOU. Rosalie, Rosalie, how could you have done this to me. I gave you everything, expensive cars, expensive jewels, I'd have given you anything you asked for if you would stop running around on me. ACK? (*LOU grabs his chest, starts choking, HE appears to be having a heart attack.*) OH! I feel it coming, it's the big one. Vinnie! Vinnie! Old Pal, I'm joining you, uuuggh ... (*LOU having distracted Hal, grabs the gun out of his hand and points it at Hal and the others.*) Got you, copper. Got you all. You thought wimpy fat Lou didn't have it in him. Well, I did, I killed him and I'd do it again. Old pal, ha. Vinnie was scum, he used people and threw them away like gum wrappers. Like he used me, first he offered me my chance to break into show-biz. Week after week he promised me I could go on, week after week he backed down. I was reduced to being the MC in this crappy dump. After ten years I knew my show-biz career was history, all I had to live for was Rosalie, then he took that away from me. Three months ago he started having an affair with her. Vinnie was running a numbers racket and not making payoffs, he was planning to run off with the mob's money and leave me holding the bag, and he was taking Rosalie with him. When Vinnie's phone was busy, and so was Rosalie's, I knew that tonight was the night for their getaway. I had to stop him ...

(*PHONE rings.*
IAN goes into his John Wayne imitation.)

LOU. I couldn't let him take Rosalie, so I killed him, stabbed him while he was sitting at his desk. Now, the club would be mine, my wife would be mine ...

BACK TO SCRIPT

IAN. (*Rising from behind sofa.*) It's the last roundup, Pilgrim ....

MURDERER "F"

BAMBY

HAL. A Piece of paper with six numbers on it. 4,4,2,8,3,6.

IAN. Someone's license plate number!

SOMNAMBULO. The combination to Vinnie's safe. 44, then 28, then 36.

HAL. That's what I thought at first too, Mr. Great. But Vinnie didn't have a safe. Then I realized it was another combination. One that someone here was counting on to get them a big payoff. Weren't they, Miss Bamby!

BAMBY. What are you talking about? I'm not any good with numbers. I can never remember my Social Security number.

HAL. These numbers you carry around with you. If you don't mind my asking, Miss Bamby, what is your chest measurement?

BAMBY. That's a girl's business and nobody else's.

ROXIE. You've been flaunting them in our face all night, why the sudden attack of modesty? Of course, 44, 28, 36. With measurements like that she deserves life imprisonment.

BAMBY. Is it my fault I'm a full-figure girl? Where is your proof?

HAL. The proof is on the paper, Miss Bamby. Along with your thumb print. You've turned your last somersault, Bamby, it's time to turn yourself in.

BAMBY. Go ahead, lock me up. I'm not sorry I did it. I'd do it again! Vinnie had it coming. He was the worst kind of slime, show business slime. He promised me a big career if I'd just make him happy. The things I had to do for that man ...

ROXIE. You, and Vinnie, it's a wonder he didn't die of a heart attack.

BAMBY. I mean, the casting couch is one thing, but the casting chair, the casting floor, the casting closet, well, you get the picture. A girl can only be so flexible. He guaranteed me the thousand bucks in this lousy contest, and then, a few weeks ago, he suddenly lost interest. He wouldn't return my phone calls, I got new costumes, choreographed new baton routines, and he wouldn't even look at them.

LOU. (*Enters.*) I got the winner, I got the winner, you'll never guess who won, I couldn't believe it myself, I had to recount ...

(LOU interrupts, BAMBY gets gun.)

BAMBY. I decided if I couldn't twirl my way to the top, or sleep my way to the top, I'd kill my way to the top. No one was gonna use me. I found out Vinnie was having an affair with another woman. A liberal and she couldn't even touch her toes. He was gonna run off with her, dumping his "little bundle of patriotism." It was down right un-American.

(PHONE rings, IAN starts to go into John Wayne imitation.)

BAMBY. I had to kill him, you see, it was like he had spit on the flag. I'm gettin' out of here, and I'm taking my batons with me. Somewhere, there is a beauty pageant that will appreciate me.

BACK TO SCRIPT

IAN. It's the last round up, Pilgrim …

HELPFUL HINTS FOR YOUR PRODUCTION

Questions and Answers
Tips for the Second Act

1. The detective is the man in control and should never let the audience or cast take the control away.

2. The Q&A portion is the key to a successful production of *Knock 'Em Dead*. It is also the most unpredictable. Therefore, your case should be quick-witted and creative. The bolder the actor, the more hilarious and outrageous it can be.

3. The character in the "hot-seat" should deny all accusations until cornered by the audience or by the detective with evidence. They can then concoct their story to cover up or explain the situation. The more far-fetched or fishy, the better.

4. If the audience does not bring up key questions, then the detective should ask the question or goad the audience into asking. Remember, no major character clue should go unexplored.

5. For the actor in the "hot-seat", this is their opportunity to have fun. They can say and do almost anything that they think will help prove that they are innocent. Stay in character, be funny, do not break the pace, and remain within the bounds of good taste. There are no limits.

6. Other cast members on stage should feel free to join in, throwing in their own questions, reminding the detective of suspicious things they saw, etc.

7. Finally, have fun. It's amazing how willing the audience will be to go along with you and how much abuse they will accept.

Each character performs a number of suspicious things during the first act which cast suspicion and provide material for quizzing in the second act.

Here are a few examples of the most commonly asked questions and examples of the loony replys the cast can provide. If audience members do not ask these key questions, then the detective or another cast member should do the asking. The cast should be reminded to exercise originality and ad-lib their own answers whenever possible. They will no doubt develop their own batch of responses that work best for them.

BAMBY QUESTIONS

Q. If you're so dumb, how come you knew those fancy medical terms for your wrists?
A. Huh? Well ... I've studied under a few doctors in my time.

Q. Why do you have that knife in your gym bag?
A. (She denies it. The detective and audience go through the bag and find the knife.) Oh! That knife! Well,

my last boyfriend was a sword swallower. The Great Expando, and he was teaching me how to swallow.

Q. How come you couldn't open the door to get into to bathroom, but you opened it to come out?
A. I'm double-jointed. I can do lots of things without my hands, if you know what I mean.

ROXIE QUESTIONS

Q. What was that phone call about?
A. What phone call? (Detective and audience remind her.) Oh! Yeah, that call … It was my mother. We were making plans to celebrate after the show.

Q. How come you said "a gun" would be too loud?
A. No, no. I'm singing at a wedding next week and she wanted an organ and I said an "or-gun" would be too loud.

Q. (From Bamby) If that was your mother how come she sounded like a man?
A. Can I help if she smokes a lot?

LOTTA QUESTIONS

Q. How did you get that blood on your scarf?
A. What blood? There's no blood on my scarf. (The Detective makes Lotta show the blood stained scarf and passes it around the audience.) Ah! The shroud of Turin!

Oh, well, I cut myself shaving my legs. I must have gotten blood on it then.

Q. If you cut yourself, show us the cut.
A. Oh, no! I couldn't do that. It's too high up!
(Roxie) No, honey, he/she said cut, (spelling.) c-u-t.

Q. Why do you keep losing your accent?
A.   I never lose my accent. It's the real McCoy. (Angrier, she loses the accent. The detective and audience catch her.) So what! I've got a fake accent. What's that mean? I just wanted a gimmick. Is that a crime? Strap a ham sandwich to my ass and send me to Ethiopia!

IAN QUESTIONS

Q. What were you doing with a book on "Knife Throwing" in that bag of yours?
A. Well, in this cut-throat business you've got to have a gimmick, and Fifi and I were working on a new act that would sure make us stars. I come out as Miss Joan Crawford strapped to a spinning target and Fifi is dressed as Betty Davis and throws knives at me.

Q. How come when the lights come back on you were trying to get into Vinnie's office door?
A. Well, when the lights went out, I was so disoriented and was feeling my way around for some tissue (you know what I mean) and thought I had found a supply closet and was trying to get in.

LOU QUESTIONS

Q. Who were you trying to call on the pay phone?
A. I never made any calls. (Audience response) Oh, that! Well when Vinnie didn't answer his door I called his number to see if it was busy and that way I knew if he was in there.

Q. What about the other calls?
A. What other calls?

Q. The ones you made to that number on the wall?
A. What number? I never tried to make another call.

Q. (Audience and detective) The number in red on the wall. You called it. Who was it?
A. Nothing! Nobody!

Q. (Detective) Well, then why don't we just call it and find out ourselves? (Searching pockets) I need a quarter. Anyone got a quarter? (He goes into the audience and begs until he has a quarter. Just as he is about to make the call, Lou stops him.)
A. Okay, so I made another call. That's my wife Rosalie's car phone number. I was trying to reach her but her line was busy so I hung up and went back to setting up the show.

Q. Did Vinnie owe you money?
A. What money?

Q. The money you said he had to come up with tonight.

A. (Panicked) No ... Ah ... I meant the money for the grand prize. That's right, the grand prize.

SOMNAMBULO QUESTIONS

Q. What was that piece of paper you had hidden in your turban?

A. What piece of paper?

Q. The one that fell out when you were leaving. (Detective) Yes, let's see that piece of paper.

A. If you insist. (Gives over the folded paper)

Q. (Detective) It appears to be a map of the club (Passes it to the audience) with a red X on Vinnie's office.

A. So what! I have a fear of fire. Whenever I work a club, I like to know where the exits are so I can make a quick get away.

Q. Why is there a big red X on Vinnie's office?

A. So that when I win the prize money, I know where to pick it up.

Q. What about the "Do Drop Inn" and your old act? (Roxie) Yeah, and your face lift?

A. I don't have to stand for this! I've never been to a pit called the "Do Drop Inn" and I have never had a face lift, and I refuse to answer any more of your inane questions!

COSTUME PLOT

LOU
Soiled white tuxedo jacket
Black tuxedo pants
Scuffed black shoes
Loud tie and cummerbund

HAL
Trench coat with pockets
Brimmed hat
White shirt
Dark pants and tie
Dark shoes

ROXIE
Rain coat with 2 large patch pockets
Loud, vulgar low-cut dress
Contrasting lace leggings
Matching shoes

BAMBY
Rain coat
Glitzy, spangled two-piece cheerleader's outfit
White spangled cowgirl boots

IAN
Over done Ice Capades outfit
Full-sleeved shirt
Sequined lace trimmed vest
Metallic stretch pants
Sequined boots

FIFI
Bright colored pull-over shirt

LOTTA
Slinky black dress w/long sleeves
Black heels
Black mesh hose
Severe black wig

SOMNAMBULO
Tuxedo pants
Ruffled red dress shirt
Gold metallic dinner jacket
Matching tie and cummerbund
Black shoes

VINNIE
White tuxedo coat with knife and blood on back
White dress shirt
Dark pants
Dark shoes
Toupee

PROPERTY PLOT

ONSTAGE
12-15 "Bud" beer cases
1 Beer case rigged for "Fifi" escape
1 Beer case with fake "Fifi" inside
Small sofa
Folding chair
Card table
Pay phone
Carmen Miranda head dress (behind sofa)

IN W.C.
Large poster announcing "Talent Contest Finals Tonight"
Lotta's blood stained scarf
Coat hook on inside of door

IN VINNIE'S OFFICE
Desk and chair
Desk dressing
Sleazy posters, photos, etc.

OFFSTAGE
Plastic ice bucket with ice
Bamby's "fried" cowgirl hat
Burnt end of Bamby's extension cord
"Winner" envelope with check

PERSONAL PROPS (brought on from Alley)

HAL BROWN
Suitcase with "Wen, Y, & Hal" on the side
Ventriloquist's dummy "Wendell"
Business card
Message from talent service

Police badge
Police revolver
Yellow "Police crime scene" tape
Note pad and pencil

ROXIE BARN
"Glow Worm" condom
Bag of snack crackers
Half-eaten Twinkie
Key on ring
Note from V.B.

BAMBY LYNN
Large dance bag
2 Batons
2 Amer. flags on sticks
Basketball
Baseball
Football
Glitzy bra
Large jeweled dagger
Locket with lock of hair
White cowgirl's hat

IAN WAYNE
2 Plastic garment bags with glitzy dresses
2 Hat boxes
Long feather boa
Hanging shoe bag with shoes
Shopping bag with:
      Silly string
      Record of "Bolero"
      Book "Knife Throwing Made Easy"
      Fake "Fifi" costume
Pink suitcase with "FIFI" in sequins on the side

2-3 Fifi costumes for act
Red high-heeled shoes
Assorted glitz, feathers, and wigs
5 ft. folding screen
Locket with lock of hair

LOTTA VERBOTEN
Long cigarette holder
3 Pieces of sheet music
5 ft. long moth eaten fur stole
Large chiffon scarf
Locket with lock of hair

GREAT SOMNAMBULO
Shopping bag with:
Oversized jeweled turban
Gold lamé cap with "G.S." on the back
Map of the Club
Book of matches from the "Do Drop Inn"

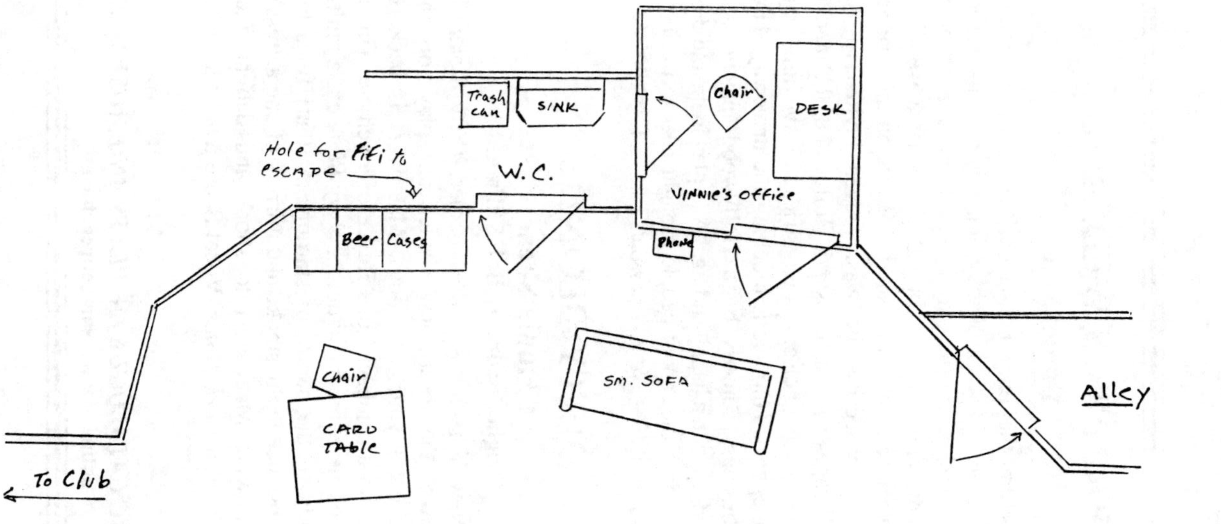

Trash can
SINK
Hole for Fifi to escape
W. C.
Chair
DESK
VINNIE's office
Phone
Beer Cases
Chair
CARD TABLE
SM. SOFA
Alley
To Club
Knock'em Dead
Ground PLAN

BARBRA'S WEDDING
Daniel Stern

The Schiffs are the only non-celebrities in their Malibu neighborhood; in fact, their shabby house is next to Barbra Streisand's mansion. As the play opens, Jerry is in a frenzy over the media circus surrounding Barbra's 1998 wedding. An out-of-work actor with one small TV role on his résumé, he resents his obscurity—he wasn't even invited to the wedding! He rages against Streisand, Hollywood, the media, his wife and everything else. His wife tries to leave him—but Schwartzennegger's Humvee is blocking the driveway. This anti-show business comedy by a Hollywood insider is a hilarious send-up with a happy ending. "A ... play in the mold of Elaine May's comedies about people brought near to madness by the quirks of life."—*New York Post*. 1 m., 1 f. (#4901)

DIRTY BLONDE
Claudia Shear
Original score by Bob Stillman

A bawdy New York hit with dream roles, *Dirty Blonde* is "hands down the best new American play of the season....Take off your hats, boys, Mae West is back on Broadway ... in a compact Rolls Royce of a vehicle. This is no evening of mere impersonation.... *Dirty Blonde* is a multi-layered study of the nature of stardom ... [that] finds the enduring substance in the smoke and mirrors of one actress's stardom, allowing Mae West to shock and delight once again."—*The New York Times*. Vocal Score available. 2 m., 1 f. (#6929)

THE BASIC CATALOGUE OF PLAYS AND MUSICALS
online at www.samuelfrench.com

CAUGHT IN THE NET
Ray Cooney

This sequel to *Run for Your Wife* finds the bigamist taxi driver still keeping two families in different parts of London, both blissfully unaware of the other. However, his teenage children, a girl from one family and a boy from the other, have met on the Internet and want to meet in person since they have so much in common—name, surname and taxi-driving dad! The situation spirals out of control as John juggles outrageously with the truth. "A master class in the art of farce.... A precession-built laughter machine."—*What's On.* "Brilliant.... The funniest play of the year."—*Daily Mail.* 4 m., 3 f. (#5865)

THE UNDERPANTS
Carl Sternheim / Adapted by Steve Martin

The renowned actor and author of *Picasso at the Lapin Agile* provides a wild satire based on the classic German comedy about Louise and Theo Markes, whose conservative existence is shattered when her bloomers fall down in public. She pulls them up quickly, but he fears the incident will cost him his government job. Louise's momentary display does not result in scandal but it does attract two infatuated men, each of whom wants to rent the Markes' spare room. Oblivious of their amorous objectives, Theo happily collects rent from both the foppish poet and the constantly whining hypochondriac. "Funny stuff ... a fine play ... with lightning flashes of wit."—*TheaterMania.com.* 5 m., 2 f. (#23042)

A Party to Murder
MARSHA KASH and DOUGLAS E. HUGHES

"Christie meets *Deathtrap* with style."— *Cincinnati Enquirer*

"Enough to turn Dame Agatha green with envy."——*Oxford Press*

"Brilliant…. Even better than *Ten Little Indians.*"—*Saskatoon Free Press*

Six people have come in secret on Halloween to play a murder mystery game at a rustic island cottage. Invited by writer Charles Prince, they are all set for a weekend of fun until ghosts from the past begin to haunt the proceedings and it becomes clear that all is not as it seems. This captivating mystery is by the authors of *Who's Under Where?* 3 m., 3 f. (#18975)

Murder at Café Noir
DAVID LANDEAU

"Mystery theatre at its finest."—*Portland Sun Times*

"It's as close as you'll ever get to stepping into Bogey's shoes at the Blue Parrot."—*Boston Herald*

"Fast and funny satire."——*Los Angeles Times*

A popular dinner show from coast to coast, this private detective story come to life features Rick Archer, P.I., who is hired to find a curvaceous runaway. His search leads him to the Café Noir on the forgotten island of Mustique. When the owner washes up on shore dead, Rick sets out to find the culprit. Was it the French madam, the voodoo priestess, the shyster British attorney, the black marketeer or the femme fatale herself? Audiences help direct Rick's investigation in this comic tribute to the black and white era of Bogey classics. 4 m., 3 f. (#15298)

Our *Basic Catalogue of Plays and Musicals* lists

**Send for your copy of the Samuel French
BASIC CATALOGUE OF PLAYS AND MUSICALS**